Christian

The God Man

Finding the Real Jesus

by
Dwight Longenecker

All booklets are published thanks to the generous support of the members of the Catholic Truth Society

CATHOLIC TRUTH SOCIETY
PUBLISHERS TO THE HOLY SEE

Contents

1. The Ultimate Revelation 3

2. Mother and Child 11

3. Actions Speak Louder Than Words 23

4. Who is This Man? 33

5. Why Did He Die? 41

6. What Did He Achieve? 50

Additional Reading 59

What to do next... 61

1. The Ultimate Revelation

If you were God what would you do? You created men and women to be your sons and daughters. You wanted them to be part of your family; you wanted them to be happy, but they turned away from you. In turning away from you their human nature became twisted. Suddenly their instinct was to hide from you.

They wanted to hide for two reasons. First, they assumed you were angry with them. Second, everything within them whispered that it would be far more fun and interesting to do things their own way.

This is what Christians mean by 'original sin'. When we say a baby is born in 'original sin', we're not saying that the baby is terribly wicked. We are simply acknowledging that every human baby will instinctively choose his own way, and that this is a flaw in their character - like a bad note in a beautiful piece of music.

When Christians say that every human being is a sinner, we are not saying that everyone is totally and

Christianity Pure and Simple

utterly wicked. Instead we are admitting the fact that, while everyone is born in the image of God, this perfect image has been distorted by selfishness, violence and greed. In other words, our goodness is stained, and we need a good scrub.

This is common sense isn't it? When we look in the mirror, or when we look at other people, we see human beings who are basically good. However in each of us there is also a shadow side. In some people the rottenness has spread and they have become more bad than good. But most of us mean well. At heart we desire what is good and true.

'Original sin' does not mean that we are rotten to the core. It means at a very basic level we are cut off from God. Instead of running towards him we are running away. Instead of looking for him we are hiding from him. One of the results of our hiding from God is that we can't see him clearly. In fact, without his help, we can't see him at all. Furthermore, all of us are in this fix together. It's a case of the blind leading the blind.

So what would you do?

Since we all have this flaw in our character we have trouble seeing what is best for us. Despite receiving good advice, we make wrong choices. The situation

The Ultimate Revelation

is similar to that of a family where the loving parents have to deal with a rebellious teenager. The parents actually know what is best, but their goodwill, patience and understanding is met with ugly, sullen behaviour. To their great sorrow, the loving parents watch the teenager constantly reject all that is best for him, and make disastrous decisions.

This is why the ancient stories in the Bible are so fascinating. The stories in the first part of the Bible (the Old Testament) tell about the relationship between the Jewish people and God. The stories are interesting not because they give us a beautiful new religion or because the Jewish people are the perfect followers of a spiritual form of life. Instead, the stories capture our imagination because they are a catalogue of human disasters. Time and again the Jewish people mess up. They reject God; they disregard his law and wind up as miserable failures.

Because their instinct was to fear God, the people of the Old Testament sometimes perceive God as being angry with his people. But we have to remember the perception of God in the Old Testament comes to us through the people of that time. God's character can only be understood according to our limited understanding.

It is true that sometimes the Old Testament God comes across as angry and vengeful, but more often he is shown to be patient and forgiving. An ancient Jewish poet says God is 'slow to anger and rich in mercy.' And through the voice of the Old Testament preachers, God cries out, 'Oh, my people, what have I done to you? What have I done to make you turn away from me?'

God sees that we are like sheep without a shepherd. We long for happiness, and we are searching everywhere to find it. At the same time, God sees that we are running from the very source of happiness, which is God himself. It is true that we are cut off from God, and our hearts are restless until they find their rest in Him. But how can God get through to us if there is a part of us that instinctively runs and hides from him? How can God reveal himself to us, if our eyes are tight shut? What would you do?

Getting through

First of all, God made sure that a hunger for goodness remained within each one of us. Because God made us, there will always be a part of us that searches for God. This is where the religious instinct in humans comes from. In fact, it is so

The Ultimate Revelation

strong that we are looking for God even when we think we are running away from him.

When we desire something beautiful, deep down we are searching for God, the source of beauty. Our desire for youth, and our fear of death and old age is really our desire for eternal life, and that too is a desire for God. When we want what is good and true, or when we cry out for justice, we are expressing our desire for God. In all these ways, at the very depth of our being, we long for God. We can't help it. It is written into our nature.

However, our natural search for God can only take us so far. Remember, there is a flaw in our nature, so that while we long for God, we also turn away from him. In a similar way we want beauty, truth, goodness and justice, but that which is totally beautiful, true, just and good also seems severe and awesome.

We long for love, and yet we are frightened of being consumed by the very love we long for. This is why all the most compelling love stories are stories of unrequited love. It is as if, like the lover in the story, we are searching for some great love, but we are blinded. Something stands in the way. We are wandering in the forest, and don't know how to find our beloved.

Making a prophet

This is why in the second part of the Old Testament the Jewish writers begin to speak the language of love. The prophets were holy men who taught the Jewish people about God in a vivid and powerful way. In many different ways the Jewish prophets tell us that God loves his people.

They say God is like a passionate lover who seeks and pursues the beloved everywhere. He is a faithful husband who loves his wife no matter what she does. The ancient Jewish writers say God is a good and gentle shepherd. He is a wise and gracious king, a patient Father, a loving mother, and a long-suffering servant.

Furthermore, the prophets said that no matter how unfaithful or rebellious the people were, God would be there. He would never be unfaithful. He might be frustrated and angry at their rebellion, but this is because he loves them and wants the best for them. The prophets say that although the people might turn away from God, he will never turn away from them.

Out of all these images of love, one image came into focus. First and foremost God revealed that he was a loving father. Furthermore, his love is unique. It is like our love, but so far greater that, in a way, it is not like our human love at all. Our love is always mixed up with false motives, fantasy and selfishness. In that sense, our love is less than real.

God's love is totally pure and real. It is a kind of love that is never selfish. It does not love the other person because it wants to be loved itself. Instead it loves the other person simply for who they are. Real love is unconditional. Real love is also active. It takes the initiative. It reaches out, and draws the loved one into an everlasting embrace.

The author steps on stage

Real love is also sacrificial. It goes to any length to bring the loved one into a loving and permanent relationship. If you really love something or someone, you will even go through pain and suffering to win that love. All along we thought God was the stern judge, a distant creator, or a vengeful tyrant, but instead God is like this: he is a vulnerable and faithful Father.

By giving us freedom to choose, God subjects himself to our will. In allowing us to run away from him God allows himself to be rejected and despised. This is a shock. It upsets all our expectations and prejudices. It is so surprising that no wonder it took two thousand years for such an astounding truth to sink in.

The message of the Old Testament prophets was that God's love was so great, that he would continue to reach out to us despite our continual rejection. To do this he planned to send a messenger to communicate his love in an unforgettable way.

We can communicate with our loved ones with letters, cards and gifts. But in the end we want to come and be with them. We want to speak to them face-to-face. This is what God chose to do. All the symbols and signs pointed to this end: God would come and visit his people.

The earlier Jewish writers said God was like a Shepherd and a King, but the later writers said the Shepherd King would appear. When the Jewish people escaped from slavery they sacrificed an innocent Lamb, but their later prophets said the sacrificial Lamb of God would come to them in a startling way.

They would no longer have to interpret vague prophecies and learn about God's love through religious writings. There would be no need to read about him in signs and symbols because all the symbols were about to be shown clearly. There was no need to read a biography; because the subject of the book was about to enter the room. The time for stories and plays were over, because the author was about to step on to the stage.

2. Mother and Child

Throughout the history of the Jewish people God was setting the stage. First of all he was showing that he is not a distant deity, but a God who is involved with real people at real places in real time. The saga of the Jewish nation 'incarnated' God. In other words, it fleshed out God's character so we could understand what he was really like by his actions.

But the Old Testament story with its symbols and signs of promise was also one huge and complex pointer to the fact that God was going to be incarnated in an even more powerful way. The story of God working in human history revealed that he was a God who got involved. If this is part of his nature, then it was a sign that he would keep on getting involved, and that one day he might intervene in human history in a fresh and astounding way.

So you can get the picture of what God was up to, let's explain the whole thing with a story. Imagine this great drama: Adam had been created in the image of God, but that image was soiled when he chose his own way instead of God's way. One of the consequences of the bad choice was that, from then on, human beings faced suffering and death.

To rescue humans from this curse of suffering and death, and to restore the divine image in them, a plan was formed. The way to rescue their soiled condition was for God himself to take human form and secretly enter their world to put things right. Where Adam had put things wrong God himself (in human form) would put them right.

For God to take human form he had to take human flesh from a real person. The natural way for this to happen is the way all of us take flesh - we are born as a baby of a human mother. But how could God take human form when all human beings were carried that fatal flaw in their nature that we call sin?

To solve the problem God intervened in a unique way when a little girl was conceived. When two ordinary people called Anna and Joachim made love God made sure that the child who was conceived was free from the distortion of original sin. This baby girl was unique among all human beings, and she is known to us as Mary, the mother of Jesus.

Mary was kept free from original sin for two reasons. First of all, God's human form had to be as fresh and perfect as Adam's had been. Second, a free choice had to be made. God couldn't force himself on Mary. She could only bear God's human form into the world by saying 'yes' to God. So she could choose freely, Mary had to be kept free from original sin.

An amazing 'yes'

Remember, one of the symptoms of original sin is that we instinctively choose the wrong way. The twist in our nature means we have a built in tendency to say 'no' to God. Because of this we are not wholly free; we have a bias towards choosing wrongly. For Mary's choice to be really free it had to be free of this bias. This didn't mean she would automatically say 'yes' to God. It simply meant that she had total freedom to choose without the built in bias that comes with original sin.

Mary's perfection doesn't mean she was some kind of superwoman. She was very ordinary. To understand this kind of perfection we need to think of something that is perfectly natural, like a forest. When you are in the forest it is beautiful and whole. Everything is working as it should work. However, that perfection seems ordinary because it is natural, and what is natural is not unusual. We don't exclaim with surprise when the sun comes up or when water runs downhill. In that same natural and wholesome

Christianity Pure and Simple

way Mary was perfect. She didn't have the flaws and distortions of character that everyone else has. She was simply all that a human woman should be.

Because of the special natural perfection that God gave her, an angel of God recognised that Mary was 'full of grace.' Grace is another word for the goodness of God, so we believe that this ordinary Jewish girl, was full of God's goodness. Because she was full of God's goodness she could perfectly co-operate with God when he asked if she would be willing to conceive and bear his Son into the world.

This fullness of goodness did not take away Mary's free will and independence. God's grace did not mean Mary was God's robot. Far from it. Instead this fullness of God's grace meant that Mary was fully human and fully free. She could have said 'no' to God when he asked her to give everything, but at that crucial moment of freedom Mary said 'yes.'

Son of God and son of man

When Mary said 'yes' to God she became pregnant, and God took real human form in the little boy Mary called 'Jesus'. The name 'Jesus' was an ordinary Jewish name from that time, but the name also means 'Saviour'. We call Jesus the Son of God, but the title he used for himself was Son of

Mother and Child

Man. Both titles are true. Because God took human form through Mary we can say that Jesus really is both the Son of God and the Son of Man. Jesus was a unique fusion of God and Man. He was totally God and totally human in the same way that you are a unique fusion of your two parents. Because Jesus is God in human form we say that Mary is 'the Mother of God.'

Christians believe that Mary remained a virgin as she conceived and gave birth to Jesus. Jesus didn't have an earthly father. Instead, by a unique miracle, Mary became pregnant by the power of God.

In the Christmas story Joseph marries Mary and helps her look after this miraculous child. Like all mothers Mary has an unbreakable link with her child. When she took him to the temple as a baby an old man told her that 'a sword will pierce your own heart also.' We know that Mary was at the cross when her son died, and so Mary was there for Jesus right through to his death. She had said 'yes' to God at the beginning and she kept on saying 'yes' to him in a perfectly whole and natural way right up to the end.

Now if you have been thinking this through at all, you should be saying, 'Whoa! Are you expecting me to swallow this?!' You really think God took human form? You believe Mary became pregnant by God? That's mind blowing!' You're right. These claims for Jesus are pretty incredible. The miracles surrounding Mary's life and Jesus' birth are not easy to believe. But stay with it. Remember, the people who lived in Jesus' time didn't find it easy to believe either, and yet certain facts occurred to make them see that these conclusions were really the only possible ones to come to.

Are miracles possible?

There are two things that make any sensible person step back with disbelief at the idea that God took human form in Jesus Christ. First of all, is the problem of miracles. Did God perform a miracle that allowed Mary to be conceived without the distortion of original sin? When Mary said, 'yes' did God perform a miracle so that she became pregnant, and did God therefore take human flesh from her? Did this incredible miracle really happen? To decide whether this is possible or not we first have to ask whether we believe miracles are possible or not. If we conclude that miracles are possible, then we have to ask whether this *particular* miracle could have happened.

As to the first question, there are really only two choices. The first choice is that the universe we live in is closed. In other words, it operates by set laws of nature that never change. If this is so, then everything can be understood by scientific observation. If the universe we live in is closed, then miracles simply cannot happen.

The other choice is that the universe is open-ended. In other words, although there are set laws of nature, the God of nature can suspend those laws if he has good reason. Which choice is more likely to be the right one? If we believe there is a God who exists above and beyond nature, and who created the natural laws, then we have to conclude (at least in theory) that God can work beyond the limits of those laws, and therefore what we call miracles can happen.

Unnatural and supernatural

Miracles are possible, but impossibilities are not possible. In other words, God may produce a miracle, but even he cannot do something that is logically impossible. He cannot make a circle square. He cannot make two plus two equal seven. A miracle, therefore, is not something that goes against nature. It is a unique and unexpected action that happens within nature.

We may wonder, for instance, how Jesus turned water into wine. In the natural cycle water turns into wine all the time. Rainwater falls and is drawn up into vines that produce grapes that are pressed into wine. Jesus' miracle didn't change nature. It simply speeded things up. How did Jesus walk on water? Walking on water is not an eternal impossibility. We can all walk on water when its frozen. Jesus didn't suspend or contradict nature; he simply shifted the way it normally works.

The same is true when we think about the miraculous conception of Mary without sin. This unique event does not go against the law of nature. It is not un-natural for a person to be sinless. Indeed, that is our perfectly natural condition. That's how we were first made. When God intervened to make sure Mary had no human flaw he was not doing something unnatural, but restoring what was most natural.

Likewise when Mary conceived Jesus without having made love to a man, God was not doing something totally un-natural or contrary to the laws of nature. Young women get pregnant. What *would* have been unnatural would be for Joseph to have got pregnant. So what happened to Mary was not unnatural. It was supernatural. In other words, a power greater than nature did something natural in a unique and unexpected way.

When you see it that way, what God did in Mary's life was no stranger than when we interfere with nature - let's say by flying in an aeroplane. Within nature we have the power to do something that goes against our nature: flying. But once we take that action, nature takes over and soon we consider flying to be quite ordinary.

This is the kind of miracle we are talking about. Because he created the natural world, God has the power to intervene in that world. God took a few unique actions within the course of nature. Just as we might use our power to change the course of natural events, so God stepped in and made a little diversion in the expected run of human history.

Can the universal become particular?

There is a second objection to this particular miracle. We rightly ask why on earth God should take a particular human form at a particular time and place. How could God do such a thing? Why would he do such a thing? Don't we all know that God is above all times and places? Isn't it a contradiction to say that he was born as a real child in a real stable in a particular village in Palestine 2000 years ago?

It sounds crazy, but when you look at it from a fresh point of view it makes sense. After all, for

Christianity Pure and Simple

anything to be real it has to become particular doesn't it? Let's say you have a good idea like, 'Every schoolchild under the age of eight should have free milk every day.' For this idea to be real, at some point in time little Harry Turnbull at St Hilda's School has to be given a pint of fresh, cold milk by Mrs Watson the dinner lady. In other words, for your idea to be real it has to become particular.

In the same way, doesn't it make sense that for God to be real to human beings he had, at some point in time, to become a human being? If God is the most real being imaginable then what would be strange would for him not to become a particular person at a particular place at a particular point in time. In fact, when you look at it this way, you could even say that God's whole existence might rely on the fact that he has to become particular. Just as you have to be born in a particular physical body to exist at all, perhaps God too, is eternally and unimaginably real because at one point he took a particular form on earth.

Science and science fiction

Despite my explanations you wouldn't be a sensible person unless you still found it all too much to take. God comes down to earth and takes human form? An ordinary girl becomes pregnant with God's son?

Mother and Child

It sounds a little bit like a science fiction story doesn't it? Where did the Christians get such a far-fetched idea in the first place?

I said earlier that they came to these astounding conclusions because of the rest of Jesus' life. Jesus came on the scene just like any other travelling Jewish preacher. In his time there were other preachers who healed people and gathered crowds around them. There were other religious leaders who had a little band of followers.

Indeed, throughout the world both before and after Jesus there have been many religious leaders who have spoken for God. In most cases their followers don't claim that they are God in human form. And yet, within a few years of his death, Jesus' disciples were teaching quite clearly that Jesus was indeed the Son of God, and that his mother was a virgin, and that he was born as the result of a miracle. Why did the disciples of Jesus come up with such astounding and incredible views?

They came to their conclusions because of what Jesus said and did during his earthly ministry. It's true that Jesus was a totally original religious teacher, but his teaching and his life carried far more meaning than just his simple and profound teachings.

Jesus' followers were Jewish, and as they examined his life in the light of the Old Testament story they came to the conclusion that he really was the Son of God. It was an astounding thing to believe and preach, but to understand why they came to that conclusion we have to look more closely at what Jesus said and did while he was on earth.

3. Actions Speak Louder Than Words

In the Old Testament the prophets were travelling preachers who spoke the word of God. But these preachers were also actors. Like any good actor they communicated by their actions as well as their words. For example, one of the prophets named Hosea married a prostitute and was faithful to her even though she carried on with lots of other men. Through his own experience Hosea was trying to drive home the point that God was like a faithful husband and the people of Israel were like an unfaithful wife.

As part of the plan, God prepared Jesus' cousin for a special ministry. This man's name was John and he was called 'the Baptiser' because he called the Jewish people to turn away from their selfish ways and return to God. As a sign of their new inwardly clean condition he asked them to be publicly washed with water. This ceremonial

Christianity Pure and Simple

washing was called 'baptism' from the Greek word 'baptizo' which means 'to wash.'

Like Hosea, John was preaching with his actions as well as his words. He wore rough clothes and lived in the desert as a sign of how terrible it was for people to live in the lonely wilderness of a life without God. To go out into the desert and be plunged into the fresh water was a sign that the person wanted to leave the desert of their sinful condition and enter a fresh, new kind of life.

But John's baptism also echoed an Old Testament ceremony. When the Old Testament king took his throne the priest anointed him for his new role. The anointing ceremony was the public proclamation of the king's identity and duty in the community.

The prophets were also anointed by God for their ministry. The symbol of having oil poured on the king or the prophet's head symbolised the blessing of God flowing down from heaven. This blessing was both recognition from heaven and the gift of power to enable the prophet or king to perform his duties.

Christ - the Lamb of God

The greatest King of the Old Testament was the shepherd boy David. The prophets predicted that

Actions Speak Louder Than Words

one day a descendent of David would come and assume the throne. He would be a new kind of shepherd King. Because the King was specially chosen by God he would have to be anointed as a sign of his special calling. The term for the 'anointed one' was 'Messiah.' In the Greek language the term for the anointed one is 'Christos' from which we get the word 'Christ.'

Once Jesus had grown up we are told that he went out to the wilderness along with everyone else to see his cousin John preaching. John had been telling the people that someone greater was about to appear on the scene. The people were full of excitement and expectation. When Jesus appeared John pointed to him and said, 'Behold the Lamb of God!'

Remember, the people considered John to be a prophet. They believed him to be a special messenger from God himself. When he pointed to Jesus and said 'Behold the Lamb of God!' the people in the crowd understood that he was referring back to the Old Testament stories. The lamb that was killed in the Passover feast was also called 'the Lamb of God.' That lamb symbolically saved the people from death, and here was John saying that this unknown preacher called Jesus was the 'Lamb of God'. What could it mean?

When John poured the water on Jesus' head it also symbolised the anointing of the promised King. To validate the anointing John heard a voice from heaven saying 'This is my beloved Son in whom I am well pleased.' Later on Jesus was given the name 'Christ' because his followers remembered how his baptism was a kind of anointing by John. When John anointed Jesus he was recognising that Jesus was the specially chosen Son of David who would be king. He was also recognising Jesus to be a specially blessed prophet and teacher. By calling him 'the Lamb of God' he was also pointing to another more mysterious dimension to Jesus' destiny.

Jesus the good teacher

Everyone will agree that Jesus was a good teacher. As such he ranks among the other great religious teachers in the world. Many of the things Jesus said are echoed in the words of other religious teachers. But while there are some similarities, there are also some big differences. Other religious teachers give their followers a plan or method to reach God. They teach a technique of prayer, or they teach their followers to obey a system of religious law or they teach a combination of both.

Actions Speak Louder Than Words

Jesus also teaches his followers to pray. However, his teaching on prayer is very simple. He doesn't teach difficult meditation techniques. He doesn't require you to undertake a course of study to master complicated religious language. Instead he teaches his followers to speak with God as a child speaks to his father.

Jesus also gives his followers a new kind of religious law. But this law is unlike any other religious system of do's and don't's. It is the law of love. He tells his followers to forgive their enemies, and to love those who do them harm. Jesus sums up all previous laws with two simple principles. First, love God. Second, love your neighbour as yourself. He says that all the religious systems in the world boil down to these two simple principles.

Jesus was an absolute genius among religious teachers. His teaching was so fresh and revolutionary that it turned the Jewish world upside down. But the most important thing about his religious teachings is not their wisdom and simple freshness, but what they reveal about Jesus himself.

Jesus the storyteller

One of the most famous ways Jesus taught people was with stories. The stories he told are called parables, and they are a unique form of story. They

Christianity Pure and Simple

do several things at once in a brilliantly simple way. They help people see how to live better lives. They show people what God is like and, like the rest of his teaching, they reveal who Jesus really is.

So, for example, Jesus told a series of stories about the final judgement. In one story a rich man gives various servants some money and asks them to invest it wisely. When he asks for the money back the various servants have to answer for what they've done, and their response varies from the brilliant investor to the fool who made no profit at all.

In the story we see how to live wisely, but we also get insight on God's character. He is the one who gives the gifts for us to use. But the story also reveals who Jesus is, because elsewhere he tells another story about the final judgement, and this time he is a shepherd judging between the sheep and the goats. (In Jesus' time sheep and goats looked very similar so judgement was difficult) As a result, Jesus' stories also revealed who he really was: the one who gives us gifts and the one who judges how we have used them.

Lost and found

Jesus also told a series of stories about things that were lost. A woman loses a valuable coin, a shepherd loses a sheep or a father loses a runaway son. In each story the person who loses something precious searches relentlessly or waits patiently, and when it is restored there is great rejoicing all around.

The stories teach us to treasure the precious things in life, but they also show us a God who never tires in his search for his lost children. But then when Jesus says he is one who comes to 'seek and to save that which was lost' the stories take on a new level of meaning, and point to his real identity.

The story where these different levels of meaning come together most powerfully is the story of the Good Shepherd who goes out to search for his lost sheep. The shepherd has one hundred sheep, but as he counts them in at the end of the day one is missing. He goes out into the wilderness to find the lost sheep and brings him home on his shoulders.

In the Old Testament the prophets had said that God was the Good Shepherd of his people, so the story reveals what God is like. But then Jesus says something that his hearers would have found shocking. He calls himself the Good Shepherd. In other words, Jesus is saying that the old promise that God himself would be the shepherd of his people is fulfilled in him.

Listen to my actions

Jesus taught his disciples to pray. He taught them to love God. He taught them with stories about life. In all these ways he was also showing them who he really was. Like the prophets before him, Jesus not only taught through his words, but through his actions. In what he said and what he did, Jesus points to the mystery of his true identity.

The miracles of Jesus are not simply the party tricks of an amazing preacher. Nor are they just Jesus' way to show that he had great power. Instead, the miracles of Jesus have a deeper meaning. They reveal who the miracle worker is. This is true for all of us. What we say, reveals our personality. But what we do, reveals our personality even more. Likewise, the teachings and actions of Jesus reveal who he is.

When Jesus taught the people, they were amazed and said, 'this man teaches with authority!' Jesus didn't disagree with them. Instead he said, that his authority had been given by God himself. When Jesus healed people from sickness, he also forgave their sins. His enemies were shocked. They said, 'only God can forgive sins!' By forgiving people their sins Jesus was making an astounding claim for himself.

When he fed five thousand people with a little boy's lunch, Jesus was doing something that only

Actions Speak Louder Than Words

God can do: multiply food to feed many people. When Jesus walked on the water and calmed the storm he revealed who he really was. The Old Testament had said that the Lord God was he 'who walks on the waves of the deep', so when Jesus walked on the waves he was revealing that he was none other than the Lord of Creation.

It is true that Jesus was a good religious teacher, but his teachings and actions led his followers to conclude that he was more than just another religious teacher. Who was this religious teacher who had the nerve to forgive sins, calm the storm, heal the sick and perform miracles to feed the hungry?

Jesus the Son of God

Through his stories, his teachings, and his actions, Jesus makes it clear that our relationship with God should be like that of a child with its Father.

But Jesus' life and teaching do more than teach us that we should be the children of God. In all his words and actions Jesus reveals what this new child-Father relationship with God should be like. Furthermore, through his words and actions Jesus is telling us that he is not just *like* God's son. He *is* the Son of God.

We might accept it if Jesus had said, 'My relationship with God is like that of a son to his

Christianity Pure and Simple

father', but he goes further than that. He says, 'I have come to do the will of my father in heaven.' And 'all authority on heaven and earth have been given to me.'

This is where the teaching of Jesus is difficult. There are many people who think Jesus is a good teacher, but those who pick out the nice and acceptable parts of Jesus' teaching often sidestep the parts of his teaching that are actually very strange and disturbing. In his teaching, in his stories and in his actions he says that he and God are one. He says this in many ways, but finally he states it quite clearly. He not only says, 'I have come to do the will of my Father.' He says, 'when you have seen me you have seen the Father', and "I and the Father are one.'

4. Who is This Man?

We wouldn't mind if Jesus were just a good religious teacher. We can accept his teachings about prayer and loving our neighbour. But can we really accept his claims to be the Son of God? We can accept that he was a good person; perhaps the greatest person who ever lived. But can we really believe that he is God in human form?

Let's stop and consider for a moment. What kind of person was Jesus Christ? If you want to know, you should sit down sometime and read through one of the gospels in one sitting. I guarantee that the Jesus you meet, will be very different from the Jesus you thought you knew.

In the Gospels we meet a man who is complex and mysterious, and yet there is no trace of those twists in personality and contradictions of character that everyone else is prone to. He goes through life with a clear purpose and stands out with a majestic simplicity and a quiet intensity that captivates and fascinates us.

He is religious, but never self-righteous. He is pure without being puritanical. He is magnificently good, but never 'holier than thou'. He is much sterner than the popular image of 'gentle Jesus meek and mild'. But while he does not tolerate one scrap of evil, he is compassionate towards those who fall into sin. He is shrewd with intelligent people, but simple with more ordinary people. He seems modest, and yet he does miracles and preaches powerfully. He is witty without being sarcastic and gentle without being weak. He is firm without being harsh, self-confident without being proud, and humble without being insecure. In every way he is balanced, mature, wise and sane.

Most importantly, in the gospels we meet someone who is honest and real to his very core. He may be complex, but he is also transparent. There is no trace of guile, self-deceit or vanity. Jesus is solid and down to earth. He doesn't strike us as a figure out of a story or a play. There is not an artificial or phoney bone in his body. Instead he has all the honest unpredictability and complexity of a real person. He knows how the world of power and influence works, but he never schemes or kow tows to anyone. He is his own man, but he is not arrogant, eccentric or proud.

When we meet Jesus in the Gospels we are confronted with a person who strikes us as being totally complete and whole. Jesus is well adjusted. He knows who he is. This is what we mean when we

Who is This Man?

say he is perfect. We don't simply mean he never did anything wrong. What we mean is that his personality doesn't have any weakness, faults or kinks. It is whole and complete. It is all that it should be. If this is so, then Jesus shows us what a totally complete and perfect human being looks like.

The image of God

Do you remember that in the story of Adam and Eve it said that the first people were created in the image of God? What it means is that Adam and Eve were created in the same perfect condition that Jesus had. That's why Christians called Jesus 'the second Adam.'

If Jesus really was whole and complete in this way, then he was a perfect human being. But if a perfect human being is created in the image of God, then he must also be a perfect image of God. This is exactly how the New Testament describes Jesus. It says he is the 'image of the unseen God'. Elsewhere it says that although Jesus was in the form of God, 'he did not consider equality with God something to cling to, but he took the form of a servant'.

The Old Testament prophets pointed to the same truth. The prophet Isaiah said that the Christ would be a suffering servant. He also said the promised one would be called 'Emmanuel' which means 'God

Christianity Pure and Simple

With Us'. The profit Ezekiel said God would be the shepherd of his people, and Jesus said he was the 'Good Shepherd.' The prophet Daniel saw a vision of heaven in which a 'Son of Man' who was as radiant and powerful as God himself sat on the throne. 'Son of Man' is the title Jesus gives himself.

In a powerful and irresistible way all the symbols and signs from the Old Testament and the New Testament come together like the pieces of a puzzle falling into place. Each sign combines with the others to build up to the conclusion that the Jesus Christ's astounding claims about himself may actually be true.

Big problems

If this is so, then the teachings and life of Jesus present us with some big problems, because all the teachings and actions of Jesus consolidate the claims that he is the Son of God.

Many people believe that 'being a Christian' means following Jesus' commandment to be good. They think it means being kind to others and trying not to lie cheat or steal. Of course, Christians should not lie cheat or steal, but being a Christian is not simply a case of trying hard to be good. At the very heart of it all being a Christian means we must come face to face with the astounding claims that Jesus Christ makes.

Put quite simply, Jesus Christ claims to be God in human form. What do we make of that? There are really only four choices. First, what do we usually think if someone claims to be God? We think he's crazy. Now it is possible that Jesus is crazy, but all the stories we have about him portray him as probably the most sane, down to earth and realistic person who ever lived.

The second choice is that Jesus is lying. Again, everything we know about him convinces us that if anyone was honest through and through, this man was. But let us suppose that he was a religious fraud. Maybe he was conning everyone. What was his motivation? There is no evidence that he gained either fame or fortune for his fraud. Indeed, he was always trying to escape from the crowds, and we know he lived in total poverty. If he was a fraud he gained nothing from it. Indeed, it caused him nothing but pain and brought him to a terrible death. Very few frauds will go so far as to die for their lie.

The third choice is that Jesus' followers made a mistake. Perhaps they misunderstood his message. Maybe they thought he was God in human form, but he never intended them to think that. There are two problems with this option. First, all Jesus' words and actions reveal that he was God in human flesh, and on several occasions he made the claim explicitly to his followers.

Second, we have to ask whether it is very likely that his followers would come up with such an outrageous suggestion. If they wanted to promote the message of Jesus, wouldn't it have made more sense to promote their friend as a great religious teacher? Once they said he was God, they made him sound not like a great religious teacher but like a madman or a fraud. In other words, even if Jesus did make such a claim, there was every reason for his followers to play it down and turn him into a good teacher instead of the Son of God.

There is one other choice. If Jesus is not a liar, if he is not insane, and if his followers did not make a mistake about his claims then there is only one other choice: he was telling the truth, and he really is who claims to be.

Who do you say that I am?

Jesus didn't allow people much leeway. He said we must make a choice. We are either for him or against him. We cannot serve two masters. We must decide whether or not Jesus really is God in human form.

We would like to defer the decision. We would like to withhold judgement, but by the nature of choice, this is impossible. We must choose, and not to choose is also to make a choice. If you are at a bus stop and a bus comes along you may choose to get on or not. If you say you are not going to choose, then that is a choice not to get on the bus.

When we are making any decision we have to be clear what the choices actually are. When we read the gospels we have to consider the claims of Jesus. When we do, the option that Jesus was just a good teacher ceases to be possible. As we have seen, he is either God in human form or he is a liar, or he is crazy, or his followers made a terrible mistake. He did not give us the option that he was just a good religious teacher.

Jesus forces this issue for a very important reason. He wants us to understand that another religious teacher is not what the human race needs. We don't need another system of good works or more techniques of meditation and prayer.

At the beginning of the first booklet we raised the difficult problem of suffering. Jesus knew that we didn't need more religion. We needed someone to wrestle with this enormous question of how God can be good yet allow suffering. Jesus understood that we need not only an intellectual answer to that question; we need someone to rescue us from the suffering each one of us is in.

Christianity Pure and Simple

In one of his stories Jesus spoke about the good Shepherd who goes out on a lonely night to find just one lost sheep. He risks his own life to save that sheep and bring him home safely. When Jesus called himself the good Shepherd he was saying that this is the reason he came - to seek and to save that which was lost.

Only God can put things right for the human race, and we can only trust Jesus to help us put things right if we believe that he has the power to do that. And we can only believe that he as the power to do that if we believe that he is God

The extraordinary claims Jesus made for himself took him right into the very heart of suffering. His claims got him into deep trouble. When Jesus was on trial he faced death because he claimed to be God. The Jewish leaders wouldn't have minded if he were a good religious teacher. They had lots of good religious teachers. What was one more? What they couldn't stand, was that he claimed to have the power of God. So they killed him. Just as he presented them with a choice, so he presents us with the same choice. And it is a choice between life and death.

5. Why Did He Die?

Rather than the end of the story, this is where the story really starts to get interesting. In the first booklet I said that the question of how a good God could allow suffering was the most important question in the whole universe. I also said that Christianity is the one religion that answers the question best. Many people think that the Christian faith simply comes up with neat intellectual answers to the problem. This is only part of the truth. The whole truth is much more terrible and glorious.

Jesus didn't come to earth simply to give us an intellectual answer to a difficult exam question. God didn't take human form in Jesus simply to fill in the blank. Instead, he came to wrestle with the problem of suffering at the heart of his very being. In Jesus God actually reaches down and embraces the terrible problem of evil and suffering in his own body.

The whole reason for his existence is shown in the story of Jesus' temptation. After he was baptised by John, Jesus went out into the desert and ate nothing for forty days. While he was in the desert he endured a terrible assault by the devil.

Wrestling with demons

Satan, or the devil, is a real spiritual being. He is an angel who has fallen from his high condition because he wanted to be like God. Demons are lesser angels who have also fallen into selfishness and seek to pervert God's way in the world.

Satan is also a symbol of death and destruction, violence and mayhem. He stands for the vast range of evil forces arrayed against all that is good. The devil also represents the evil that each one of us struggle against. When he grappled with the devil, Jesus was not just trying hard not to do anything bad. He was beginning a battle with evil that would last for the rest of his life.

His wrestling match with the devil was a picture of what Jesus' whole life was really about. He did not come simply to teach people about God. He was not on earth just to heal people and teach them how to pray. His main purpose was to answer the problem of evil once and for all - not by teaching about evil, but by fighting a terrible battle against the devil to the very death.

The unfair advantage

If a good person decides to fight against evil he will always be at a disadvantage. He is fighting uphill for three reasons. First, because the good person is good he has to fight evil. The good person has to engage with evil. He is not allowed to be a pacifist and sit on one side.

The good person is disadvantaged for a second reason. Because the evil person is evil he will naturally use every devious and nasty trick he can think of. That's why he's bad in the first place: he is a liar, a cheat, a murderer and a thorough scoundrel.

There is a third disadvantage for the good person: because he is good he cannot use the same evil tricks. So the evil one will lie and scheme. He will punch below the belt and throw salt in the good guy's eyes. But the really good person is not allowed to lower himself to dirty tricks. Jesus actually taught this principle. When our enemy slaps us we are told to turn the other cheek. When our enemy takes our coat we are to offer him our shirt as well.

This disadvantage that the good person suffers is actually the key that unlocks the whole mystery. You see, evil gets worse and worse in the world because we do not fight it with goodness. We usually respond to suffering by causing more suffering. We seek revenge and return evil for evil.

When we do this, evil breeds in the world and will never be defeated. That is why Jesus teaches us to return good for evil, to forgive our enemies and pray for those who hurt us. Jesus is trying to get across to us that the only way for evil to be defeated is to smother it with goodness as water puts out a fire.

The sacrificial lamb

That sounds neat and tidy. It's not. We forget how evil the enemy really is. If we turn the other cheek and refuse to fight evil with more evil, then by the very nature of that decision we will become victims of evil. The violent ones will have no qualms about squashing good people under foot.

Despite this, the answer is not to return evil for evil. The only answer therefore, is for the good person to become the victim of evil. Therefore the stark answer to the problem of evil seems to be that the forces of evil must trample the good person down, and the good person must become an innocent victim.

In the Old Testament religion, this is what the sacrifice of an innocent lamb was supposed to symbolise. The pure little lamb did nothing wrong. He was put forward as symbol of innocence in the face of evil. He was unable to fight against evil, so the evil forces would devour him. He would be slaughtered and die.

When the Jews celebrated Passover they actually slaughtered the 'Lamb of God' and daubed its blood on their doorways so that the powers of death would pass over their home and they would be delivered. In a symbolic way they believed the innocent lamb took the evil of the world into itself. Evil was absorbed into goodness, even if it meant that the goodness would have to die and the light would have to be put out.

Jesus Lamb of God

All of this is gathered when Jesus takes the title, 'Lamb of God.' Because he is good, Jesus must battle against evil. But because he is good he is not able to fight evil with evil. He cannot return violence for violence. As a result, the violent will bear him away.

The battle against evil is grim, and the price is great. When Jesus was betrayed by friends, condemned by a crooked court and crucified with criminals he shows us that real goodness is devoured by evil. There is no other way. Because the evil one cheats, lies and uses violence he wins.

But at the very darkest point the tables are turned. The Jewish people celebrated the Passover not as a celebration of defeat, but a celebration of liberation. Through the Passover events they came out of slavery and began their journey to the land of prosperity and promise.

In the same way, when Jesus is trampled down and finally killed by the powers of evil, the tables are turned. Although evil must win the battle, good must win the war.

When faced with the darkest evil we must always remember something that the evil ones always forget: that evil has no real power of itself. Evil is only good twisted and perverted. At the heart of evil is a dark void. Because evil is nothing positive in itself it cannot possibly triumph in the end. Likewise, because goodness is positive and powerful, it must finally prevail. Darkness may seem overwhelming, but darkness is nothing in itself. It is simply the absence of light. Therefore even the smallest amount of light must banish the dark.

The powers of evil may have been able to snuff the light of Christ, but they could not put out the light forever. How could evil *really* win? It is

Why Did He Die?

impossible because evil (since it is a twisted good) actually relies on goodness for its very existence. It evil were to win; if the devil could kill God, then he would be cutting off the branch he was sitting on. Because evil is dependent on good for its existence, if good is vanquished, evil itself would also cease to exist.

It was inevitable that Jesus would be trampled by the powers of evil, but he couldn't stay have stayed dead if he wanted to. Because Jesus was God, and because of his overwhelming goodness, he had to rise again just as surely as the rooster has to crow and just as surely as the sun will rise each morning. Goodness had to prevail. That is how the whole system is written.

The death and resurrection of Jesus are therefore the ultimate answer to the question of suffering and a good God. Because he is good, God creates a universe where freedom exists. This means evil is a possibility. Evil twists the natural order. It distorts what is good. As a result terrible suffering follows. This suffering goes in a downward spiral away from goodness, away from what is natural, and away from God. But because God is good he himself provides the solution, even though it costs him everything.

Christianity Pure and Simple

A cause to celebrate

This is why Christians celebrate Holy Week and Easter as the most important part of the year. Each year we celebrate the fact that Jesus Christ defeated evil not with the tools of evil, but by his overwhelming goodness - even though that meant his own terrible death.

On Easter Day we celebrate the historical fact that Jesus could not stay dead. Death could not hold him. He was too alive, too good, and too powerful for that. His ultimate sacrifice meant that he embraced death and evil and simply squeezed them to death with his overwhelming love and goodness. That's why he rose from the dead, because there was simply no more death to hold him.

This is the heart of the Christian faith. To become a Christian we don't just listen to Jesus and try to be good. Instead we come to understand the meaning of his death and resurrection, and we participate in that same victory. When a person becomes a Christian they accept what Jesus' death means and they are baptised as a symbolic way of entering into that death.

This is also what Christian worship is all about. We don't go to church just to meet our friends, sing hymns and hear the good teachings of Jesus. We go to participate in his victory over evil. Through the ceremony of the Mass or the Eucharist, Jesus' death and resurrection come alive in the present moment and we re-live them with Christ.

At that point we celebrate the amazing fact that the eternal riddle of evil and a good God has been answered once and for all. The war is over. The victory is won. All that remains is for us to sign the peace treaty and put it into force.

6. What Did He Achieve?

When the first Christians reflected on the death of Jesus they came to some revolutionary conclusions. As Jews, the followers of Jesus considered Adam to be a representative of the whole human race. The word 'Adam' means 'man', so when they said Adam was created in the image of God the ancient writers meant all of mankind was created in God's image. If Jesus really was a new and even fuller image of God in human form, then it was right to call him 'the second Adam'.

According to the story, the first Adam brought death and suffering into the world by his disobedience, but the second Adam (Jesus) defeated death and suffering through his total obedience to God's will. The New Testament says Jesus was obedient 'even to death on the cross.' Through his terrible death Jesus wrestled with suffering and death for the whole human race.

It is difficult for us to put ourselves into the same mindset as these first Christians two thousand years ago. We think individuals are most important and find it difficult to understand how one person can represent the whole human race. Its quite sensible to ask, 'How can the death of Jesus affect me two thousand years later?'

But if you look at things in a fresh way it is not that difficult is it? In political terms we all understand how a head of state like a queen or a president can represent the whole nation. Also, the scientists tell us that we have all descended from the same genetic parents. In one sense we really are all connected. We are all brothers and sisters in the human race. If this is so, then any human could stand for the whole human race.

But God didn't choose just any person. He chose the person who was a totally whole, complete and perfect human being to represent all of us. Because he was whole and totally complete as a human being, Jesus Christ held each one of us in himself. So when he embraced suffering and death Jesus really was embracing the suffering and death of each one of us.

Justice and mercy

It is very difficult for us to conceive how the death of Jesus can touch us. But there are many ways to think about it. Saying he represents the whole human race is one way. But we can also think about where we were headed, and what it took to turn us around.

Christianity Pure and Simple

Because of our twisted human condition all of us are on the road away from God rather than towards him. This, by its very nature, means we are headed for disaster. It is not so much that God is punishing us because we are naughty little children. Instead, our punishment is built into our decision. Our choice to disobey God has within it, the choice to be separated from him forever. If we go our own way we mustn't be surprised if we end up far away from God.

God realises that we are headed away from him, and he doesn't want us to end up in such a disaster. But because God is good he must also be just. He can't just take away the natural results of our bad choices, otherwise the choices themselves would be meaningless. So God has to allow justice to take its course.

But because God is good he is not only just. He is also merciful. Therefore God must make sure justice is done while mercy is exercised. So in a brilliant stroke, God has seen fit for his own son to offer the human race both justice and mercy at the same time.

When Jesus died on the cross Christians believe that God himself took the just punishment for our disobedience and offered us mercy in return. It is not that Jesus died in our place to satisfy an angry God. Instead Jesus stepped in to make God's justice effective while he also offered mercy. Part of this mercy means that, if we want to, we can turn away from our selfish path through life, accept what Jesus has done for us and turn back toward God.

Forgiveness forever

Another way of talking about God's mercy and justice is with the term 'forgiveness.' We often think of forgiveness as simply excusing somebody for an injury. So when someone steps on our toe we say, 'Don't worry, I forgive you.'

But when we are really hurt badly, forgiveness isn't so easy. The person who stepped on our toe didn't mean to hurt us. It was an accident. But if that person not only steps on our toe, but does so deliberately time and again, then we do not forgive quite so easily. If we do forgive, we are right to demand restitution. If he has broken our toe we might forgive him, but we still want him to pay the doctor's bill.

When Jesus died on the cross Christians believe he won God's forgiveness for all of us. He did this by paying the price of our forgiveness, and that price was the death and suffering that was required for evil to be defeated forever.

Christians therefore say that 'Jesus died to save us' or 'Jesus died to forgive us'. This is what it means in theory, but this is also what it means in reality. The forgiveness and mercy Jesus won on the cross really is available for individual people. The way to obtain this forgiveness is the way we always obtain forgiveness: By asking for it.

Good, bad or forgiven?

This is the simple and astounding truth: Christianity is not about being good. It is about being forgiven. A Christian comes to realise who Jesus Christ is, and what he has accomplished through his death and resurrection. Once he has realised this, he uses various means to connect with that death and resurrection and claim the results of it for himself.

The simplest way to do this is to simply face facts and say to yourself, 'I have been living my life my way. It hasn't brought me real happiness. I want to live life God's way.' Once we've come to that realisation all we need to do is pray, 'Dear God, I want to live life your way. I want to claim forgiveness and mercy from Jesus Christ. Please help me.'

At its heart, this is what it means to be a Christian; to hear the call of Christ and decide to follow him. Down through the ages this simple decision has been taken by billions of people. Little children as well as old people have taken that decision. They have done so in the midst of a church service, in a moment of crisis, at confession, or through the rituals and ceremonies of the Christian faith.

Sometimes they have done so with great emotion and felt a huge surge of love and new life in their lives. Other times they have done it with quiet confidence and simple trust. However they have done it, these billions of people of every race, language and tribe down through the ages have simply heard the call of Jesus Christ, and they have dropped what they were doing, turned from their own way and followed him.

Transformed into his likeness

It is true that Jesus calls us to follow him, but he also says, 'you cannot be my follower unless you take up your cross and follow me.' In other words, following Jesus means not just trying to live by his teachings, but to become like him. Jesus wants us to live in union with him, and to live his life in the world.

This means we are called not just to be religious people, but transformed people. Christians are not just following religious laws and techniques for prayer and meditation in order to be better people. They are seeking to be totally and utterly transformed into the image and likeness of Jesus Christ.

Christianity Pure and Simple

Jesus Christ was totally who he was created to be. He shows us humanity at its richest and fullest potential. To be like him, therefore, is for each one of us to become all that we can be, and, while remaining ourselves, to be re-created into the image of God - just as God first intended.

This is where forgiveness leads us: to a basic turnaround from walking our own way to walking in God's way. Walking our own way is like a downward spiral into nothingness. Walking God's way is an upward climb into the fullest and richest life imaginable. This climb isn't easy, but it is the goal we were created for, and unless we are on this upward climb we are not becoming all that we can be.

Just as Jesus was the God-Man, so when he calls us to be like him the call is to be no less than little God-men and women. The New Testament puts it another way. It says our ultimate destiny is to be brothers and sisters of Christ - the adopted sons and daughters of God. The exciting news is that he has also given us the power to accomplish this transformation.

Theory and practice

This is not just nice religious talk. This is not just theory. It is practice. It can really happen, and this total transformation of individuals into little god-

What Did He Achieve?

like beings is the whole point of the Christian religion. For this to happen Jesus Christ established a practical way for us to become one with him and for this transformation of ourselves, and eventually the whole human race to begin.

Jesus did four things. First he set up a community of like-minded people. Everyone who wanted to join this community had go through the initiation ritual of baptism. In this ceremony they declared their desire to turn from their own way, they expressed their belief in Christ and vowed to join his continuing fight against evil in the world.

Second, Jesus established a basic ceremony through which this community would always remember his death, because (as we have seen) his suffering and death were the heart of the whole matter. Through this ritual Jesus promised to remain with his followers forever and to fill their lives with his own life and power.

Third, Jesus set up a visible and historical structure for this community. It was simple in its design. Twelve men would be leaders by Christ's own appointment. As the community grew, they would appoint successors. So they would know who was in charge, Jesus chose one of those men, named Peter, to stand in Christ's place as the main leader.

Finally, he promised to be with his followers until the end of time. To do this he sent his own spirit into the world to be the Life Force of this fledgling community. The exciting way that Great Holy Spirit transforms our lives and changes the world is the subject of the next booklet: *The Fire of Life - Who is the Holy Spirit?*

Additional Reading

The Holy Bible - try and obtain a Catholic Edition or one which contains the 'Apocrypha'. The Jerusalem Bible or New Revised Standard Versions are good translations.

The four *Gospels* are also available from CTS at only £1.00 each.

The Catechism of the Catholic Church

Christian Classics
Mere Christianity by C.S. Lewis
The Screwtape Letters by C.S. Lewis
Orthodoxy by G.K. Chesterton
The Everlasting Man by G.K. Chesterton
The Creed in Slow Motion by Ronald Knox
Early Christian Writings by Maxwell Staniforth
The Penguin Dictionary of Saints by Donald Attwater and Catherine Rachel Jones

Modern Catholic Books
Catholocism for Dummies by J Trigilio and K Brighenti. 'For Dummies' is a highly successful series in plain English, without being patronising or simplistic.

Catholic Lives by Greg Watts - a collection of stories of people who have become Catholic.

The Path to Rome by Dwight Longenecker - a more weighty collection of conversion stories than *Catholic Lives*.

More Christianity by Dwight Longenecker - this book explains the Catholic faith in a friendly way to non-Catholic Christians.

Adventures in Orthodoxy by Dwight Longenecker - a witty and colourful exploration of Christian belief.

Exploring the Catholic Church by Marcellino D'Ambrosio - a good small introduction to the Catholic Church today.

What Catholics Really Believe by Karl Keating - exploration of the Catholic faith in a question and answer format.

Knowing the Real Jesus by David Mills - a well written exploration of what the first Christians thought about Jesus Christ.

Surprised by Truth by Patrick Madrid - three volumes of American conversion stories.

Where is that in the Bible? and *Where is that in Tradition?* by Patrick Madrid - easy to read Catholic answers written in a punchy style.

What to do next...

You can order one or all of the other books in the CTS Christianity Pure & Simple series:

1. Is Anybody There? (Ref Do 699)

2. The God Man (Ref Do 700)

3. The Fire Of Life (Ref Do 701)

4. The Great Battle (Ref Do 702)

5. Welcome Home (Ref Do 703)

The quickest way to order is to call CTS direct on 020 7640 0042

You can send us a fax if you wish, on 020 7640 0046

Or pop your order in the post to:
CTS, 40-46 Harleyford Road,
Vauxhall, London SE11 5AY

Or visit our website
www.cts-online.org.uk/pureandsimple.htm

If this book has interested you and you want to discover more about Christianity then you may also find useful the following list of organisations:

www.faithcafe.org

If perhaps you already have some familiarity with the Catholic Church, but would like to explore some of the themes you've read about in this series, your local church may run Catholic Faith Exploration or CaFE

Catholic Enquiry Office

For enquiries about becoming a Catholic, knowing more about the Church or finding your local parish church. 114 West Heath Road, London NW3 7TX; Tel: 020 8458 3316; Email: ceo@cms.org.uk